THE GLASS HOUSE

THE GLASS HOUSE

Introduction by PAUL GOLDBERGER

Essay by PHILIP JOHNSON

NATIONAL
TRUST
FOR
HISTORIC
PRESERVATION®

LINCOLN
KIRSTEIN
TOWER

GHOST
HOUSE

LIBRARY/
STUDY

CALLUNA

DA MONSTA

ENTRANCE
GATE

POPEST

GRAINGER

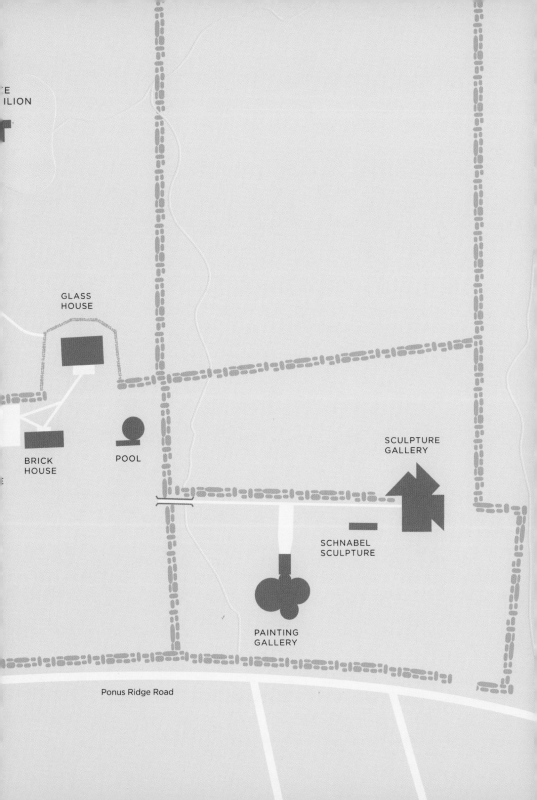

INTRODUCTION   Paul Goldberger

Philip Johnson did not achieve one of his wishes, which he expressed to his biographer, Franz Schultze, thusly: "I will work until I am 100. Then I will move to Rome." But Johnson came close to attaining this and most of his other hopes. When he died in January, 2005, a few months short of his 99th birthday, he was at the Glass House, the extraordinary compound of his design in New Canaan, Connecticut that, if not Rome, surely deserves to rank as one of the great works of American domestic architecture. The Glass House—the name of the original structure has come to connote the entire compound—is a set of buildings that would have assured Johnson a significant place in the history of American architecture had he done nothing else.

Philip Johnson, of course, did quite a bit else. He designed buildings ranging from other modernist houses in New Canaan to museums, skyscrapers, commercial and institutional buildings in a variety of architectural styles around the world, in a career that lasted almost to his death. Some of his buildings, like the New York State Theater at Lincoln Center (now the David H. Koch Theater), the AT&T (now Sony) Building in New York, Dumbarton Oaks Museum in Washington, and the Transco (now Williams) Tower in Houston are memorable chapters in recent architectural history. Though Johnson was not by any means our greatest architect, the serene beauty of the Glass House notwithstanding, he was in many ways the most important presence in American architecture for much of the second half of the twentieth century. It is no exaggeration to say that he, more than anyone else, shaped the architectural life of our time, as a curator, scholar, and public presence. His curious, energetic, and mercurial mind possessed an almost unquenchable passion for architectural ideas, and when that was combined with his determination to have an impact on the broader culture, extraordinary things happened. It began with his early explorations of modernism in Europe with Henry-Russell Hitchcock in the nineteen-twenties, which yielded the book *The International Style* and the exhibition of the same name at The Museum of Modern Art in

1

1932, twin events that made European modernist architecture visible for the first time in a significant way in the United States. Philip Johnson was part and parcel of The Museum of Modern Art almost from its founding. He was the museum's first curator of architecture, and he organized some of its most important exhibitions, including one that gave Mies van der Rohe his first serious attention in the United States, and another, "Machine Art," that showed how willing he was to break through traditional barriers separating industrial design from the realm of high art.

He pursued the new as naturally as a moth moves to light. His corner table at the Four Seasons in midtown Manhattan, the restaurant he designed in 1958 that remains the standard by which all other modern restaurants are judged, was the site of a *de facto* architectural seminar that met every day at half past noon. Sometimes his guest would be a client or another famous architect, and sometimes it would be a journalist with whom he wanted to share the latest gossip, but just as often the guest would be a younger architect whose work he had heard about and who he was determined to get to know. Architects like Robert Stern, Frank Gehry, Charles Gwathmey, Richard Meier, David Childs, Peter Eisenman and Jaquelin Robertson were among the many who began to lunch with Johnson when they were young, and remained regulars at his table until close to the end of his life.

But for all that Johnson did, it is inevitably to the Glass House that one returns. His identity is so tied into this place that the structure feels less like a work of architecture than an autobiography written in the form of a house, much like Jefferson's Monticello or Sir John Soane's Museum in London— amazing buildings in which the architect was the client, and the client was the architect, and the goal was to express in built form the preoccupations of a life. In Johnson's case, the preoccupation might almost be considered a series of embraces of different ideas.

The Glass House itself, built in 1949, is essentially one room, fifty-four feet long and thirty-two feet wide, with only a brick cylinder containing a bathroom rising to the ceiling. From inside, the carefully manicured landscape visible through the glass functions as an enclosure, and the ironic illusion is superb: The vistas tell the occupant that he is open to the whole world, while in truth there is no world outside at all, just the elegantly arranged landscape that is as much a part of the house as the furniture. The line between inside and outside becomes both visually and conceptually ambiguous. Modernism opens you to the world—sort of.

When this house was new, it seemed startlingly radical—nothing like it had ever been seen before. (The Farnsworth House, Mies van der Rohe's masterwork in Illinois, which like the Glass House also now belongs to the National Trust for Historic Preservation, had already been designed—Johnson knew the designs well—but it had not yet been built.) Often, people did not know what to make of the Glass House. There is a wonderful story of a woman coming to visit it, looking about, and saying rather snottily, "Well, it may be very beautiful, but I certainly couldn't live here."

"I haven't asked you to, madam," Johnson is said to have responded.

It is hard not to compare the Glass House to the Farnsworth House, but despite the obvious similarities, the two are hardly the same. The Farnsworth House, for one thing, is a single building, a place representing the ultimate expression of architectural genius at a moment in time, whereas the Glass House is part of an estate created over 50 years, showing us the evolution of a fertile, active, and passionate intelligence over the course of a career.

But even if we talk only of the Glass House itself and compare that single building to the Farnsworth House, there are still essential differences. The Farnsworth House is white and asymmetrical; it appears to float above the ground, and space moves beneath it. The Glass House is black and symmetrical, and it sits foursquare on the ground, almost like a classical temple. What you can see in the Farnsworth House is Mies van der Rohe expressing the modernist desire to break free, to break free of the rules of gravity and the rules of architecture, and to rewrite it all: to find a new, higher form of serenity, to make a composition of subtle purism. But here in the Glass House, Philip Johnson was saying something else. He wanted to come back to earth, so to speak, to reconnect to the history of architecture, to show that the most pristine and elegant and modern of buildings did not have to rewrite all the rules. The Glass House both celebrates Mies van der Rohe, and begins to move away from him.

If there is truly such a thing as a public intellectual, Philip Johnson was a kind of public aesthete. His stock in trade was his endless willingness not just to engage with ideas, but to try to build them. And nowhere do we see that more clearly laid out than in the whole sequence of buildings on the Glass House grounds: first in the Glass House itself, then in the brick Guest House, whose interior Johnson redesigned in a manner influenced by the British nineteenth-century classicist Sir John Soane; then in little pavilion floating on a pond, a remarkable trick of scale that came from his decorative classicism phase; then in the remarkable underground art gallery of 1965, whose hanging, swinging panels were also influenced by Soane; and the spatially active, energetic sculpture gallery, which Johnson built in 1970. It did not, of course, stop there: after these others came the white* library/study, a kind of primal hut; the Kirstein Tower, an homage to Johnson's longtime friend Lincoln Kirstein; the "ghost house," made of chain link fence and a nod to Frank Gehry; and finally, a much more elaborate homage both to Gehry's later work and to the architectural visions of the painter Frank Stella, the deep red, curving metal building by the front gate, which Johnson named "Da Monsta."

By the time "Da Monsta" went up in 1995, Johnson had already given the estate to the National Trust for Historic Preservation, retaining the right for him and his companion, David Whitney, to continue to live there for the rest of

---

* The Library/Study was painted a soft brown color in 1997 which was selected by Johnson in consultation with color experts Donald Kaufman and Taffy Dahl. Kaufman later noted that "no name was ever given" and described the color as "stone greige."

Johnson's life. Whitney died just six months after Johnson, at age 66, and like Johnson left a significant bequest to support the ongoing preservation of the property. The Glass House opened to the public in 2007, a centerpiece of the National Trust's larger efforts to protect modernist buildings and draw attention to them as a critical part of the national architectural heritage. When planning for the future of the Glass House as a National Trust Historic Site began, the expectation was that "Da Monsta" would serve as a visitors' center, where visitors would be welcomed to the property and given a brief overview before walking down the curving driveway to the Glass House itself. That proved impossible when the Town of New Canaan, concerned about the impact of automobile traffic in its residential streets, required that the National Trust locate the visitors' center away from the estate and in the commercial center of town. It turned out to be just as well, since it avoided the intrusion of a parking lot onto the grounds, and it allowed the "Da Monsta" to be more of a pure folly, a building put up solely for pleasure.

But that, of course, is what the entire estate is: a series of architectural explorations and mental entertainments—or is it a series of architectural entertainments and mental explorations? Either way, this is an extraordinary record of a great architectural mind, operating with curiosity, inventiveness, and passion, not to mention a degree of freedom that is rare in any age. It could not have been built by anyone but Philip Johnson, and there is no place else like it.

PAUL GOLDBERGER 2011

THE GLASS HOUSE   Philip Johnson

My place in New Canaan is a kind of "diary of an eccentric architect." I have kept this diary for almost fifty years starting with the purchase of the land in 1946. When I first walked over the original five-acre section (the property today is around forty acres) I sited The Glass House where it is today. The contortions I went through before I actually built the house in 1949 are recorded elsewhere, but the setting on the hill I picked in the first five minutes.

For the last forty years I have gradually, in bits and pieces, made a landscape punctuated by little buildings grouped casually in mown fields marked by farmers' stone walls and decorated by trees in rows, in clumps, in leafy copses conveniently watered by a brook and a pond. How much of this landscaping is the fortuitous use of the existing fields and forests and how much is inspired by my love of English eighteenth-century landscape gardening, I have no idea.

Since 1950 the diary continues with the sometimes chameleonlike quickness of my changes of approach to the art of architecture. The first revolt from "modern" was the 1953 intervention in the Guest House of a double-domed skeleton of a room within a room. The aim of the design was to arrange the light sources from outside the "room" as in the breakfast room in Sir John Soane's house in London.

That change did not affect the landscape. More radical was the Pavilion—the folly—"floating" in a pond I excavated in the valley below the house in 1962. The design is a false scale pavilion (you might hit your head in the arches) made up of 8-foot squares arranged more or less like a Mondrian. I derived the "toe-ing" of the columns from Delaunay's famous painting of the Gothic church of St. Severin. He spread the lower part of the columns, a motif that I utilized in later buildings in Nebraska and New York. My main concern, however, was to create a corner column that would keep the module without the Renaissance problem of "disappearing" columns in the interior corners of the arcades.

The third addition is the Painting Gallery, added in 1965, on land north of the original five acres. Since I did not intend to add new buildings too close to The Glass House, I made a berm around it. The cloverleaf shape of the gallery was a result of the functional solution: a central column in each "leaf" carrying a screen for pictures, like a Rolodex or a postcard rack. Different-sized circles provided three differently scaled picture-hanging "walls." The entrance to the almost underground "Kunstbunker," as it was called by critics, is similar to the "Tomb of Atreus" in the Peloponnesus, Greece: solemn and important.

Down the path from the Painting Gallery came the Sculpture Gallery of 1970. Even farther from The Glass House, its white painted brick stands out in the bucolic surroundings. This time I played with interlocking volumes, the roof being 45 degrees offset from the floor. The gabled roof is diagonal to the floor layout. This building is "modern," perhaps, but there is the idea of the plan—a central court with four bays opening out—which is surely classical. The floors of these bays are on five different levels, however, depending on the type of sculpture to be displayed.

Then comes the later addition to the south, a white stucco studio of 1980. A monk's cell by intent, it has a vaguely Islamic look due to a domelike truncated cone over the worktable and a minaretlike chimney in one corner. A single small window allows one to observe the weather and Nature (Frank Lloyd Wright always capitalized Nature).

In 1984 I built below the Studio a 15-foot by 15-foot construction of galvanized chain-link fencing in honor of my friend Frank Gehry, who favors using this material. Lilies grow inside, while the omnivorous deer are kept out. The building is architecturally a fantasy, symmetrical with a 45-degree pitched gable, as a child would sketch a house. It sits romantically on a nineteenth-century footing of a cow barn now long gone (the pleasures of ruins!).

In 1985 I designed a tower dedicated to Lincoln Kirstein. Placed in the landscape to make a point of interest, it punctuates the panorama from the house. The tower is in actuality a very steep and precarious stairway.

In all my recent work I strive for nostalgia, precariousness, sexual yearning. I am not sure whether or not Freud could have fun with these peculiar impulses, but I always hope some of these feelings can be transferred to stone and steel.

In the lake pavilion, for example, the small scale gives the visitor a feeling of all-importance, superiority over the environment. The fact that the Pavilion is an island gives a romantic feeling of impregnable solitariness. My footbridge to the art galleries is quite scary: too narrow and springy. You might fall off? The Glass House: the glass might shatter in the wind! In the Lincoln Kirstein Tower there are no railings on the stairs. Again, you might fall off! All these feelings must be, of course, faint. A truly dangerous situation would be counter-attractive and counter-architectural.

The tower is built of concrete block, a not beautiful but cheap and, for my purposes, perfect material since I needed a small module that could give scale and make my staircase precarious.

As I write in the winter of 1993, on the drafting board is what may be the last building on my property. I am planning a small parking lot with an attendant tower building to create a Visitors' Center when the owner of the property, the National Trust for Historic Preservation, takes over. The design was begun a year after my Deconstructivist Exhibit of 1988 at The Museum of Modern Art. I was much influenced by the work of these young (to me) men and women. The result is the present design, my appreciation of some of influences of these "kids," as I have been calling them.

The diary is probably complete. There are some new ideas floating in the peculiar recesses of my mind but there may not be the opportunity to build them here.

Anyhow, I do not need any new architecture here. I like it the way it is.

PHILIP JOHNSON 1993

Preface to *Philip Johnson: The Glass House,* edited by David Whitney and Jeffrey Kipnis

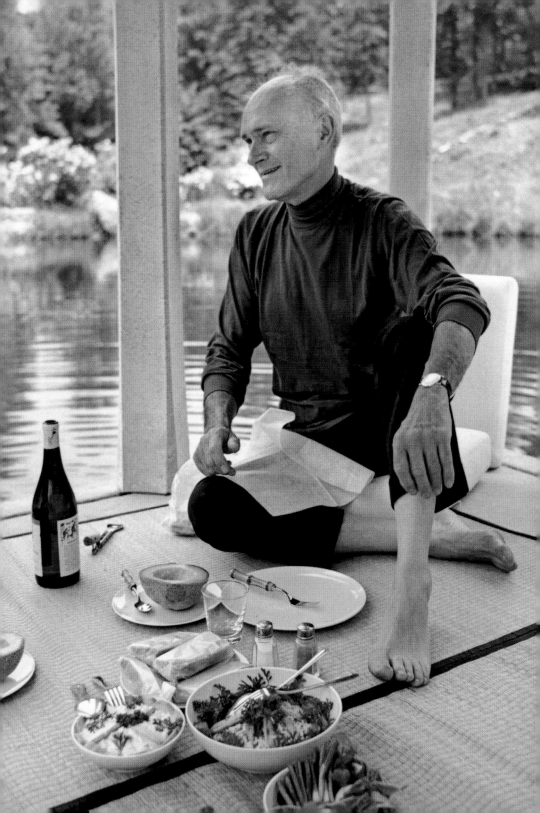

CHRONOLOGY

1906   Philip Johnson born on July 8 in Cleveland, Ohio

1923   Enters Harvard College, concentrating in history and philosophy

1928–1930   Travels throughout Europe visiting modern architects, including J. J. P. Oud, Walter Gropius, Ludwig Mies van der Rohe, and Le Corbusier, at times accompanied by Alfred H. Barr, Jr., and Henry-Russell Hitchcock

1930   Graduates from Harvard College

1930–34   Appointed the first Director of the Department of Architecture at The Museum of Modern Art (MoMA), NY

1932   Organizes *Modern Architecture: International Exhibition* at MoMA with Henry-Russell Hitchcock and publishes *The International Style: Architecture Since 1922*

1939   David Whitney born on March 28 in Worcester, Massachusetts

1940   Philip Johnson returns to Harvard to study architecture under Marcel Breuer and Walter Gropius

1943   Receives Bachelor of Architecture from Harvard University, Graduate School of Design

1945   Begins schematic design of the Glass House

1946   Purchases five acres in New Canaan, CT

1946–54   Returns to position as Director of the Department of Architecture at MoMA

1947   Finalizes design of the Glass House

1948   Groundbreaking for the Glass House and Brick House

1949   The Glass House and Brick House completed

1953   Brick House interior remodeled

1955   Pool completed

1957   Johnson purchases Popestead

1958–2005	Johnson serves as a Trustee at MoMA
1960	Whitney and Johnson meet
1962	Pavilion completed
1965	Painting Gallery completed
1968–71	Johnson serves as a Trustee at the National Trust for Historic Preservation
1970	Sculpture Gallery completed
1971	Site-specific untitled sculpture created by Donald Judd
1977	Entrance gate completed
1980	Library/Study completed
1981	Whitney purchases Calluna Farms
1981–2005	Calluna Farms remodeled
1984	Ghost House completed
1985	Lincoln Kirstein Tower completed; Brick House bathroom remodeled
1986	Philip Johnson donates the Glass House to the National Trust for Historic Preservation, retaining a life estate
1989	Whitney Garden at Calluna Farms completed
1990	Whitney purchases Grainger
1995	Da Monsta completed
ca. 1996	Popestead remodeled
ca. 1999	Grainger remodeled
2005	Philip Johnson dies at age 98 on January 25
2005	David Whitney dies at age 66 on June 12; as directed, his New York and Connecticut estates support the National Trust for Historic Preservation's preservation and programming of the Philip Johnson Glass House
2007	The National Trust for Historic Preservation opens the Philip Johnson Glass House to the public

Philip Cortelyou Johnson 1906–2005

Philip Cortelyou Johnson was born in Cleveland, Ohio in 1906. Following his graduation from Harvard's Graduate School of Design in 1943, Johnson designed some of America's greatest modern architectural landmarks. Most notable is his private residence, the Glass House, a 47-acre property in New Canaan, Connecticut. Other works include: the Abby Aldrich Rockefeller Sculpture Garden at The Museum of Modern Art, numerous homes, New York's AT&T Building (now Sony Plaza), Houston's Transco (now Williams) Tower and Pennzoil Place, the Fort Worth Water Garden, and the Crystal Cathedral in Garden Grove, California. An associate of Ludwig Mies van der Rohe in the 1950s, Johnson worked with the modern master as the project architect on the Seagram Building and the design of its famed Four Seasons Restaurant.

Before practicing architecture, Johnson was the founding Director of the Department of Architecture at The Museum of Modern Art (MoMA) in New York. His landmark 1932 exhibition, on the *International Exhibition* (later published as *The International Style*), introduced modern architecture to the American public. Johnson continued a relationship with MoMA throughout his life as a curator, architect, trustee, and patron. He donated more than 2,200 works of art to the Museum including works by Andy Warhol, Jasper Johns, and Robert Rauschenberg.

Johnson was a singular tastemaker, influencing architecture, art, and design during the second-half of the twentieth century. He referred to the Glass House site as his "fifty-year diary."

David Grainger Whitney 1939–2005

David Whitney met Philip Johnson in 1960 when Whitney, a student at the Rhode Island School of Design, attended a lecture Johnson gave at Brown University. Whitney's visit to the Glass House a few weeks later marked the beginning of a 45-year relationship that ended with Johnson's death in 2005. More than domestic, their relationship was a creative partnership in which

Johnson focused on architecture and Whitney was the deciding influence on the art the two men acquired.

A curator, collector, and passionate advocate of contemporary art, Whitney organized major exhibitions of Jasper Johns, Cy Twombly, Franz Kline, and Willem de Kooning. In 1979, he organized *Andy Warhol: Portraits of the 70s*, the controversial installation which featured deep red walls and a tower containing Mao portraits. In the 1980s, Whitney's attention turned to younger artists including Michael Heizer, Julian Schnabel, and David Salle. A compulsive collector, Whitney's wide-ranging taste included George Ohr pottery, Tiffany glass, and furniture by Elizabeth Garouste and Mattia Bonetti.

Whitney was a protector of artists and a man of fierce loyalties. He formed close friendships with Andy Warhol (to whom he spoke daily), Jasper Johns, Cy Twombly, Andrew Lord, Steve Wolfe, and Brice Marden. An avid gardener, his influence is evident throughout the Glass House landscape from the subtly sculpted meadows, to the peony garden at Grainger, and the succulent garden at Calluna Farms, which he based on the drawing *Suprematist Composition* (n.d.) by Kazimir Malevich.

Glass House Main Pavilion

Designed 1945–48; completed 1949.
Glass and painted steel; 1,728 sq. ft.

The Glass House is best understood as a pavilion for viewing the surrounding landscape. Invisible from the road, the house sits on a promontory overlooking a pond with views towards the woods beyond. Each of the four exterior walls is punctuated by a centrally located glass door that opens onto the landscape. The house, which ushered the International Style into residential American architecture, is iconic because of its innovative use of materials and its seamless integration into the landscape. Philip Johnson, who lived in the Glass House from 1949 until his death in 2005, conceived of it as half a composition, completed by the neighboring Brick House.

Since its completion in 1949, the building and decor have not strayed from their original design. Most of the furniture came from Johnson's New York apartment designed in 1930 by Mies van der Rohe. In fact, Mies designed the iconic Glass House daybed specifically for Johnson. A seventeenth-century painting attributed to Nicolas Poussin graces the living room. The image, *Burial of Phocion*, depicts a classical landscape and was selected specifically for the house by Alfred H. Barr, Jr., the first director of The Museum of Modern Art. The sculpture *Two Circus Women* by Elie Nadelman is an original artwork that was later used as a model for the enlarged marble sculpture that is found in the New York State Theater at Lincoln Center, designed by Johnson in 1964.

Nicolas Poussin, attributed to, 1594–1665

Burial of Phocion, 1648–1649
Oil on canvas; 50 x 62 in.

Nicolas Poussin defined French Baroque classicism in painting. With the exception of two years serving as court painter to Louis XIII, Poussin spent his entire career in Rome, where he specialized in allegorial paintings—scenes from ancient history, mythology, and the Bible—notable for their dramatic clarity and nobility of purpose. *Burial of Phocion* depicts the funeral of an Athenian general put to death because he refused to conceal the truth. The idealized landscape is a memorial to Stoic virtue.

Acquired at the suggestion of Alfred H. Barr, Jr., founding Director of MoMA, and a permanent fixture in the Glass House's main pavilion since its construction in 1949, the painting remains one of only two artworks on view in the Glass House (the other is a sculpture by Elie Nadelman). The installation of *Burial of Phocion* in the Glass House reveals Johnson's love of landscape and was a source of inspiration to Johnson as he designed the Glass House landscape. His childhood on an Ohio farm, with its spatial stability and rational order, is manifested in the Connecticut property in the studied placement of pavilions and buildings and the selective removal of trees. The painting serves as a mediator between the interior geometry of the Glass House and the tamed exterior landscape seen through its transparent walls.

Brick House

Designed 1945–48; completed 1949. Interior remodeled 1953. Bathroom remodeled 1985.
Brick and wood frame construction; 988 sq. ft.

The Glass House and the Brick House offer a lesson in contrasts. Designed at the same time, the Brick House was completed a few months before the Glass House. A grassy court links the two buildings conceived of as a single composition. Both houses are 54 feet long; however, the Brick House is only half as deep as the Glass House. The Brick House contains all the support systems necessary for the function of both buildings. As opposed to the transparency of the

Glass House, brick almost completely encases the house. The only windows, with the exception of the skylights, are large circular forms at the rear of the building. According to Philip Johnson, this series of round openings alludes to Filippo Brunelleschi's fifteenth century Duomo in Florence.

Johnson remodeled the interior of the Brick House in 1953. Originally there were three equally-sized guest rooms, but now a narrow skylit corridor connects a bedroom and reading room. The low, sleek, white vaults that decorate the bedroom are based on the breakfast room of the Sir John Soane House in London completed in 1824, and are harbingers of elements later found in Johnson's original design of the synagogue for the Congregation Kneses Tifereth Israel in Port Chester, New York and later at Lincoln Center. The room is covered in a patterned silk fabric designed by Fortuny. The wall relief sculpture *Clouds of Magellan* was commissioned from Ibram Lassaw for this room. Prints by Brice Marden line the corridor, and the reading room consists of Johnson's library of philosophy, history, art history, biographies, travel guides, fiction and reference books. The Brick House is temporarily closed for renovation.

Pavilion

Completed 1962.
Pre-cast concrete; exterior 6.5 ft. high; arch apex 5.3 ft. high.

In 1962, Philip Johnson completed a small pavilion on a man-made pond below the Glass House. Johnson liked to bring guests to the Pavilion for lunch parties. Visitors would sit on cushions beneath the gold-leafed ceiling of the Pavilion and enjoy the mist and sounds from a fountain originally in the center of the pond and the smaller fountains in the structure.

In the tradition of architectural follies in garden design, the Pavilion's scaled down size plays with the viewer's sense of perspective, making it seem further away than it actually is. This interest in scale stemmed from Johnson's knowledge of Italian architecture, especially the work of Baroque architect Francesco Borromini and his Mannerist predecessor Giulio Romano. In an essay published in the 1963 book, *Full Scale False Scale*, Johnson wrote about his curiosity with the effects of architectural scale.

The Pavilion represents an exploration of ideas realized in Johnson's design of the New York State Theater at Lincoln Center (1964) and the home of the New York City Ballet. With the Pavilion, Johnson also applied the architectural ideas of Walter Gropius concerning prefabricated elements and used the pavilion to investigate the Renaissance problem of how best to handle corners created from columns.

Painting Gallery

Completed 1965.
Masonry and earth berm construction; 3,778 sq. ft.

Philip Johnson designed the Painting Gallery to house the collection of large-scale modern paintings that he and David Whitney collected throughout their lifetimes. Works by Frank Stella, Andy Warhol, Robert Rauschenberg, David Salle, Cindy Sherman, and Julian Schnabel hang in the Gallery.

The exterior of the Gallery is a grass-covered mound, topped by a low parapet with a monumental stone entrance. Johnson claimed the Treasury of Atreus (c.1250 BC), a tomb located in Mycenae, Greece, was his inspiration. The stone flanking the entranceway is red sandstone. While certainly a reference to antiquity, Johnson designed the painting gallery at a time when artists such as Walter de Maria and, later, Michael Heizer were creating earthwork sculptures, which also possibly influenced Johnson's thinking. Johnson designed similar underground bermed structures in 1965 such as the Geier House in Cincinnati, Ohio.

The parapet traces the Painting Gallery's interior plan of three circles of various diameters. Circular *PK33* stools inside the Gallery designed by Poul Kjaerholm echo this motif. In each of the circular rooms, there is a rotating "poster-rack" for displaying two paintings per spindle. Although Johnson preferred to see six works at a given time, this device allowed for the storage of 42 paintings. Originally, Johnson thought this could be a model for a small museum, but later realized that security issues would make this arrangement impractical.

Frank Stella 1936–

Darabjerd I, 1967. Fluorescent acrylic on shaped canvas; 120 x 180 in.

Over the course of several decades, Philip Johnson amassed one of the most extensive collections of work by Frank Stella. Fourteen major pieces by Stella spanning the years 1960 to 1990 and representing eleven separate series are found on the Glass House property. Philip Johnson was an avid, early collector of Stella and he donated Astoria (1958) to the Museum of Modern Art. It is a transitional work that preceded the "Black Painting Series" with which Stella emerged on the New York art scene in 1959.

Stella was among the first artists of the twentieth century to spend his entire career working within the realm of abstraction. He began with striped paintings distinctive for their integral logic and reductive natures, then moved, in series after series, into increasingly irregular and elaborate structures and progressively improvisational modes of working. Eventually, his works came to assume fully sculptural dimensions.

Sculpture Gallery

Completed 1970.
Brick cavity wall construction; 3,650 sq. ft.

Philip Johnson's inspiration for the Sculpture Gallery was in part the Greek islands and their many villages marked by stairways. Johnson remarked that in these villages, "every street is a staircase to somewhere." The building's plan comprises a series of squares set at 45-degree angles to each other. Staircases spiral down past a series of bays, which contain sculptures by artists, in the following visual sequence: Michael Heizer, Robert Rauschenberg, George Segal, John Chamberlain, Frank Stella, Bruce Nauman, Robert Morris, and Andrew Lord. A final chamber tucked below the entrance holds another Chamberlain sculpture and three works by Frank Stella.

The building's glass ceiling is supported by tubular steel rafters that contain cold cathode lamps. Sunny conditions reveal an extremely complex pattern of lights and shadows in the building's interior five levels. The structure so pleased Johnson, he seriously considered moving his residence from the Glass House to the Sculpture Gallery. However, as he quipped, "Where would I have put the sculpture?"

Donald Judd 1928–1994

Untitled, 1971; concrete.
Minimum height 36 in.; maximum height 48 in.; outside radius 150 in.; inside radius 132 in.

Donald Judd, a leading figure in Minimal Art, abandoned painting in the mid-1960s in favor of the creation of three-dimensional objects that he called "specific objects." These strong geometric forms utilized industrial materials to convey complex thoughts and ideas.

The Glass House was home to many works by Donald Judd that over the years were donated to The Museum of Modern Art. Judd's *Untitled*, 1971, is the single remaining piece,

a site-specific work that is embedded in the landscape and an important part of the site's unfolding experience. The driveway leading from the Entrance Gate pivots around the sculpture, leading visitors to the central pavilion of the Brick House and Glass House.

This work is Judd's first outdoor concrete site-specific installation.

The sculpture is made of reinforced concrete, and takes the form of a large ring or circle with straight sides that is open in the middle. The interior circumference is a horizontal plane, while the exterior circumference runs parallel to the sloping ground, creating a beveled edge. Judd's solid concrete ring plays against the transparency of the Glass House and the masonry pattern of the Brick House, sharing the fact that each presents a single geometric shape. When viewed in conjunction with the circular pool, added in 1955, the sculpture completes Johnson's asymmetric composition of sliding rectangles and circles within the Glass House's historic core.

Andy Warhol 1928-1987

Philip Johnson, 1972.
Acrylic and silkscreen inks on canvas; 96 x 96 in.

Andy Warhol, a successful commercial illustrator in the 1950s, began to print images derived from comic strips and advertisements in 1960. By 1962, he was a leading Pop artist who used the silkscreen process to transfer photographic images derived from the mass media and popular culture to canvas. Philip Johnson and David Whitney were among his most important supporters. Johnson donated several major paintings, among them the iconic *Gold Marilyn Monroe* (1962), as gifts to The Museum of Modern Art. Johnson frequently commissioned Warhol to create works for buildings he designed, the most famous example being *Thirteen Most Wanted Men* intended for the New York State Pavilion at the 1965 World's Fair. Due to Governor Nelson Rockefeller's objections to its content, Warhol had it covered with silver paint. David Whitney organized the exhibition *Andy Warhol: Portraits of the 70s*, in 1979 for the Whitney Museum of American Art.

The single major Warhol remaining in the Painting Gallery is a portrait of Philip Johnson from 1972. This painting, which repeats the same pensive image of the architect nine times in a grid format, is rendered in a subdued, earth-tone palette.

Library/Study

Completed 1980. Masonry construction; 384 sq. ft.

This structure, a one-room workspace and library, was referred to by Johnson as an "event" on the landscape. From the Glass House, it is approached through a field of tall grass and wetlands. When first completed, the Library/Study's stucco exterior was bright white, but later Johnson painted it a soft brown color, which he was reluctant to give a name. "It's an emotion, not a color," he claimed. The color was selected in consultation with color experts Donald Kaufman and Taffy Dahl.

The interior walls are lined with bookcases filled with volumes on architecture, from nineteenth century tomes on German architecture to more recent publications on the work of Mies van der Rohe, Le Corbusier, and J.J.P. Oud. The selection of books demonstrates the scope of Johnson's architectural interests, from broad surveys of European, Japanese, Islamic, American, and ancient architecture to monographs on contemporary architects. Books on Johnson were maintained in separate spaces elsewhere on the property.

Johnson liked to sit and read in the interior niche, facing a small window that looks out at the nearby Ghost House. He commented that he had specifically designed the space to be a comforting "monk's cell." While the space has a fireplace, it has no bathroom. Primary lighting comes from a skylight located in the conical dome.

Ghost House

Completed 1984. Chain link and steel; 346.5 sq. ft.

The Ghost House is an architectural folly, a playful structure that sits atop a nineteenth century stone barn foundation. It is an ode to the work of two very different architectural directions. The chain-link material employed was influenced by Frank Gehry's use of everyday materials, while the overall form of the structure references

Robert Venturi and Denise Scott Brown's design methodology which reference the iconic form of a house—a rectangular base topped by a peaked roof. It is not a functional shelter.

Philip Johnson described this construction as "the spirit of a classical house." It was built at the height of his interest in postmodernism, a style that, among other things, celebrated traditional forms.

Entrance Gate

Completed 1977. Concrete and aluminum construction; 20 ft. 4 in. high

The Entrance Gate was the result of years of planning. Referencing medieval gates, this entrance to the property was primarily a ceremonial monument marking the beginning of a journey. Flanked by two twenty-foot tall concrete forms, a system of electronic pulleys raises and lowers a metal bar either to permit or prevent vehicles from entering the driveway. Da Monsta, the last structure to be built on the property, sits just behind the gate.

First painted white, the gate was later changed to a plum-brown color chosen by Johnson and Whitney with the help of color experts Donald Kaufman and Taffy Dahl.

Lincoln Kirstein Tower

Completed 1985. Painted concrete block; 30 ft. high

Built in 1985 and named after a close friend, the Lincoln Kirstein Tower was intended to be an "event" on the landscape. The tower is to be viewed and scaled. Johnson liked to climb the structure, which he described as "a staircase to nowhere." There is an inscription at the summit of the tower, which Johnson refused to reveal to visitors. Johnson felt the design, based partly on the geometry of dominoes and on the choreography of Balanchine, was in line with his attitude towards "safe danger." The proportions of the steps are designed to foster a sense of imbalance.

Philip Johnson's friendship with poet Lincoln Kirstein began in the 1920s when the two were undergraduates at Harvard. At that time, Kirstein founded the Society for Contemporary Art, a group that exhibited works of early modern art, many years before the establishment of The Museum of Modern Art. While at Harvard, Kirstein also developed a literary magazine, *The Hound and The Horn*, that celebrated writers such as James Joyce, Gertrude Stein, and T. S. Eliot.

Kirstein would later pour his energies into the world of dance, beginning with Sergei Diaghilev's Ballet Russes and later with the work of George Balanchine. Kirstein was seminal in bringing Balanchine to New York to start the School of American Ballet and later to form the New York City Ballet. Johnson designed the home of the New York City Ballet, the New York State Theater for the Performing Arts.

Da Monsta

Completed 1995. Modified gunite construction; 990 sq. ft.

Philip Johnson was a friend and supporter of both Frank Gehry and Peter Eisenman—the influence of both seems evident in the non-Euclidean form of Da Monsta. However, Johnson claimed that his original inspiration for Da Monsta was the design for a museum in Dresden by artist and close friend Frank Stella. In fact, when Johnson first made a model of this structure, he named it "Dresden Zwei," or "Dresden Two," and presented it to Stella.

Always steeped in history, Johnson also cited the work of German Expressionist Hermann Finsterlin as a source of inspiration. Finsterlin was known for fantastic designs that stretched the limits of architectural form. German Expressionism, an early twentieth century movement, had influenced Johnson's thinking on architecture in the past. In particular, he claimed that his Crystal Cathedral in Southern California was also the outgrowth of re-examining Finsterlin.

This building is the closest to Johnson's thinking about sculpture and form at the end of his life—what he called the "structured warp." This architectural direction using warped, torqued forms is far from the rectilinear shapes of the International Style.

The name of the building is an adaptation of "monster," a phrase for the building that resulted from a conversation with New York Times architecture critic Herbert Muschamp. Johnson felt the building had the quality of a living thing.

CREDITS

Entrance Gate.
(Courtesy of Patrick Hentsch-Cowles)

East and North Façades, Glass House.
(Courtesy of Eirik Johnson)

Site plan.
(Courtesy of Pentagram)

Living Room, Glass House.
(Courtesy of Eirik Johnson)

Driveway to site-specific
sculpture by Donald Judd.
(Courtesy of Patrick Hentsch-Cowles)

The Glass House, 1964. *From left to right*:
Andy Warhol, David Whitney, Philip Johnson,
Dr. John Dalton, and Robert A.M. Stern.
(Courtesy of David McCabe)

Philip Johnson on the promontory, 1964.
(Courtesy of Bruce Davidson and Magnum Photos)

Interior of the Glass House looking North,
featuring the sculpture *Two Circus Women*
by Elie Nadelman and the painting *The Burial
of Phocion* attributed to Nicolas Poussin.
(Courtesy of Paul Warchol)

Bedroom, Glass House.
(Courtesy of Eirik Johnson)

Study, Glass House.
(Courtesy of Eirik Johnson)

Corridor, Brick House.
(Courtesy of Dean Kaufman)

South Façade, Glass House.
(Courtesy of Paul Warchol)

View of Lincoln Kirstein Tower and
the Pavilion from the promontory.
(Courtesy of Eirik Johnson)

View from eyebrow bridge across the meadow
and grass courtyard towards the site's historic
core, the Glass House and Brick House.
(Courtesy of Paul Warchol)

IInterior of the Pavilion, 1963.
(Courtesy of the Estate of Ezra Stoller and Esto Photographics, Inc.)

Philip Johnson picnicking in Pavilion, 1964.
(Courtesy of Bruce Davidson and Magnum Photos)Photos)

View East toward Brick House.
(Courtesy of Patrick Hentsch-Cowles)

Andy Warhol and David Whitney in the guest bedroom, Brick House, 1964. (Courtesy of David McCabe)

Path to the Pavilion.
(Courtesy of Dean Kaufman)

Lincoln Kirstein Tower.
(Courtesy of Carol Highsmith)

Guest bedroom, Brick House. Johnson
commissioned Ibram Lassaw to create
the sculpture, *Clouds of Magellan*, for
the bedroom. (Courtesy of Dean Kaufman)

Entrance, Painting Gallery.
(Courtesy of Paul Warchol)

Interior, Painting Gallery. Paintings by
Frank Stella (*left*) and David Salle (*right*).
(Courtesy of Paul Warchol)

Ghost House.
(Courtesy of Carol Highsmith)

Interior of the Ghost House.
(Courtesy of Paul Warchol)

Interior, Sculpture Gallery. Sculptures (*from top,
counter-clockwise*) by Michael Heizer, George
Segal, Robert Morris, and Bruce Nauman.
(Courtesy of Julius Shulman and Juergen Nogai)

View from the Ghost House facing east.
(Courtesy of Paul Warchol)

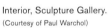

View of the Sculpture Gallery from Southeast.
(Courtesy of Richard Payne)

Interior, Sculpture Gallery.
(Courtesy of Paul Warchol)

Da Monsta.
(Courtesy of Paul Warchol)

Library/Study.
(Courtesy of Paul Warchol)

View of the Glass House at night
from the pool. Exterior lighting
designed by Richard Kelly.
(Courtesy of Robin Hill)

Detail of books, Library/Study.
(Courtesy of Robin Hill)

Interior, Library/Study.
(Courtesy of Robin Hill)

View East towards the promontory.
(Courtesy of Eirik Johnson)

Johnson on the promontory, 2002.
(Courtesy of Richard Payne)

ACKNOWLEDGMENTS

The Philip Johnson Glass House would like to thank Paul Goldberger for his generous contribution to this book. We also wish to thank the following individuals and organizations for their gracious permission to use their images: Richard Payne and Amy Ladner; Michael Bierut, Jim Biber, and Yves Ludwig of Pentagram, New York; Bruce Davidson and Magnum Photos; Inc.; Eirik Johnson; David McCabe and Susan Cipolla; Paul Warchol of Paul Warchol Photography, Inc.; Patrick Hentsch-Cowles; Dean Kaufman and Julian Richards, LLC; the Estate of Ezra Stoller and Esto Photographics Inc; Julius Shulman & Juergen Nogai; Robin Hill of Robin Hill & Company, Photography; Carol Highsmith of Carol M. Highsmith Photography; the Arnold Newman collection; Getty Images; Frank Stella; Sotheby's; Judd Foundation; Visual Artists and Galleries Association, Inc.; Andy Warhol Foundation for the Visual Arts; Artists Rights Society (ARS), New York; and Tim Lee.

MISSION STATEMENT

The Philip Johnson Glass House, a National Trust Historic Site, offers its 47-acre campus as a catalyst for the preservation and interpretation of modern architecture, landscape, and art; and as a canvas for inspiration, experimentation, and cultivation honoring the legacy of Philip Johnson (1906–2005) and David Whitney (1939–2005). For more information visit www.philipjohnsonglasshouse.org.

NATIONAL
TRUST
FOR
HISTORIC
PRESERVATION·

The National Trust for Historic Preservation is a non-profit membership organization bringing people together to protect, enhance and enjoy the places that matter to them. By saving the places where great moments from history—and the important moments of everyday life—took place, the National Trust for Historic Preservation helps revitalize neighborhoods and communities, spark economic development, and promote environmental sustainability. With headquarters in Washington, DC, nine regional and field offices, 29 historic sites, and partner organizations in all 50 states, the National Trust for Historic Preservation provides leadership, education, advocacy, and resources to a national network of people, organizations, and local communities committed to saving places, connecting us to our history, and collectively shaping the future of America's stories. For more information visit www.PreservationNation.org.

First published in the
United States of America in 2011
by Skira Rizzoli Publications, Inc.
300 Park Avenue South
New York, NY 10010
www.rizzoliusa.com

p. 59 (top): Courtesy of Arnold Newman / Getty Images; p. 59 (bottom): Courtesy of David McCabe; p. 62: Courtesy of Carol Highsmith; p. 63 (bottom): Courtesy of Sotheby's / Artists Rights Society (ARS), New York; p. 65 (top): Courtesy of Art © Judd Foundation. Licensed by VAGA, New York, NY. Photo Courtesy of Carol Highsmith; p. 65 (bottom): Courtesy of © 2007 Andy Warhol Foundation for the Visual Arts / Artists Rights Society (ARS), New York; p. 66 (bottom): Courtesy of Carol Highsmith; p. 67 (top): Courtesy of Tim Lee; p. 67 (bottom): Courtesy of Dean Kaufman; p. 68 (bottom): Courtesy of Paul Warchol

2012 2013 2014 / 10 9 8 7 6 5 4 3 2

Distributed in the U.S. trade by
Random House, New York

Printed in the U.S

ISBN Hardcover: 978-0-8478-3816-5
ISBN Paperback: 978-0-8478-3824-0

Library of Congress Control Number: 2011930062

FOR PHILIP JOHNSON GLASS HOUSE,
A SITE OF THE NATIONAL TRUST FOR
HISTORIC PRESERVATION:
Project Manager: Rena Zurofsky
Editor: Hunter Palmer
Editorial Assistants: Emily Leibin, Kate Lichota

FOR SKIRA/RIZZOLI INTERNATIONAL
PUBLICATIONS:
Editorial Coordinator: Allison Power
Design: Sara E. Stemen
Design Coordinator: Kayleigh Jankowski